R.E.M. AROUND the sun

T0040930

WWW.REMHQ.COM

Project Manager: CAROL CUELLAR
Book Art Layout: JANEL HARRISON
Album Art: © 2004 R.E.M./Athens, LLC

CONTENTS

AFTERMATH

Words and Music by
PETER BUCK, MIKE MILLS, MICHAEL STIPE

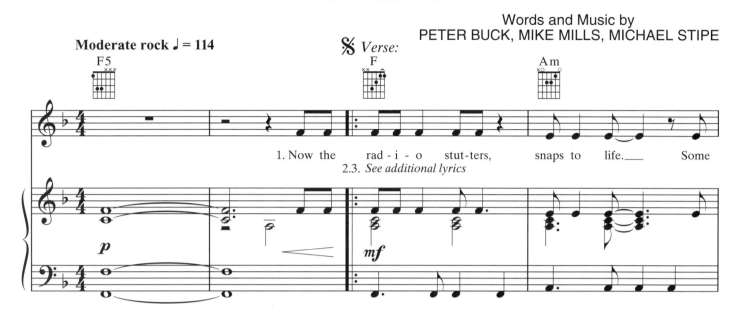

1. Now the rad-i-o stut-ters, snaps to life.___ Some
2.3. *See additional lyrics*

so-ur song___ that set's it right.___ And when Lon-don falls___ he'd

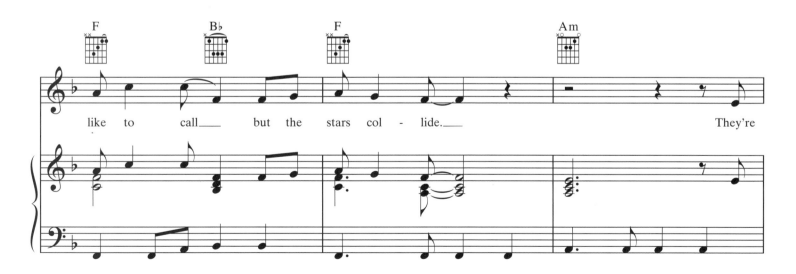

like to call___ but the stars col - lide.___ They're

6

and you see it all.____

Verse 2:
It's easy to dismiss the "What's it all about" crowd.
There is no doubt. It's this, here, now.
And you close your eyes.
He's not coming back.
So you work it out, overfeed the cat.
And the plants are dry and they need to drink.
So you do your best, and you flood the sink.
Sit down in the kitchen and cry.
(To Chorus:)

Verse 3:
Now the universe left you for a runner's lap.
It feels like home when it comes crashing back.
And it makes you laugh
And it makes you cry,
When London falls and you're still alive.
The radio stutters, it makes you laugh
And the aftermath,
Open up your eyes,
You're so alive.
(To Chorus:)

AROUND THE SUN

Words and Music by
PETER BUCK, MIKE MILLS, MICHAEL STIPE

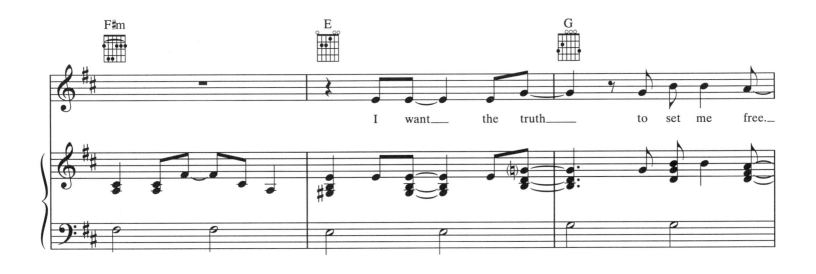

10

BOY IN THE WELL

Words and Music by
PETER BUCK, MIKE MILLS, MICHAEL STIPE

1. Look at this, it's me__ walk - ing a - way.__
2.3. *See additional lyrics*

Look at you, drown - ing, on dis - play.__ Ev - 'ry time I've dropped by,

I've tried to say__ the wa - ter is ris - ing, you don't want to stay.__ It's that

Verse 2:
The track mall gang went off
On the Tennessee goth, a lunar moth,
You chrysalis and flail.
The water is rising. You try to rappel.
A rousing cheer for the boy in the well.
(To Pre-chorus:)

Verse 3:
Here is where I look back.
Here is where you fell.
This is where I got up,
Shaking off my tail.
This is where your rope trick
Started to look stale.
A greyhound pass for the boy in the well.
(To Pre-chorus:)

ELECTRON BLUE

Words and Music by
PETER BUCK, MIKE MILLS, MICHAEL STIPE

Moderately ♩ = 98

Verse:

1. You're on your ear,___ the o- cean's near,___ the light has start- ed to fade.___ Your

high is timed,___ you found the climb.___ It's hard to fo- cus on more___
who am I?___ I'm just a guy.___ I've got a sto- ry like ev-

3. *See additional lyrics*

Verse 3:
So, bide your time
You'll feel the climb
Your high, it builds like a lightning storm.
It sings like pearls
You know that girl
And no one is any the wiser so, as if on cue, electron blue.
(To Chorus:)

FINAL STRAW

Words and Music by
PETER BUCK, MIKE MILLS, MICHAEL STIPE

Chorus:

Then I raise my voice up high-er and I look you in the ___ eye. And I of-fer love with one con-di-tion, with con-vic-tion, tell me why, tell me why.

I WANTED TO BE WRONG

Words and Music by
PETER BUCK, MIKE MILLS, MICHAEL STIPE

Verses 2 & 3:

2. Now, I know that the sun___ has shined___ on my___
(3.) ro - de - o is staged,___ gold cir - cle, goat___

___ side of the street,___ the bas - ket of A - mer - i - ca,___ the wee-
___ rop - ers and clowns.___ A rum - ble in the third act; tie 'em up___

vils and the wheat.___ The milk and hon - eyed con - gre - ga - tion,
___ and burn 'em down.___ We're armed to the teeth;___

scrubbed and ap - ple - cheeked,___ sa - lute A - pol - lo Thir - teen from the rat -
born a lit - tle breech.___ Blue - plate spe - cial an - a - lysts,___ cells___

Choruses 2 & 3:

HIGH SPEED TRAIN

Moderately ♩ = 90

Words and Music by
PETER BUCK, MIKE MILLS, MICHAEL STIPE

Verse 1:

1. When I look in-to your eyes, you drop like an an-chor eyes. I scud-ded and clipped the sky, just shy of mak-ing it.

§ *Verses 2-4:*

2. And you al - most got a - way.
3. And you caught me on the sly.
4. I'll bring you a big bou - quet.

I told you I was a - fraid.
You've tak - en me by sur - prise.
I picked it my - self to - day.

Did I real - ly want to try?
You've mir - rored my best dis - guise.
It com - ple - ments your eyes.

and turned it back on me.
You're hold - ing me to my claim.
There's love at the end of the line.

Chorus:

I jump on a high - speed train.____ I'll never look back____ a - gain.____ I flail like the an - te - lope____ who____ jumped from the build - ing. jumped from the build - ing.

Chorus: I jump on a high - speed train.__

42

LEAVING NEW YORK

Words and Music by
PETER BUCK, MIKE MILLS, MICHAEL STIPE

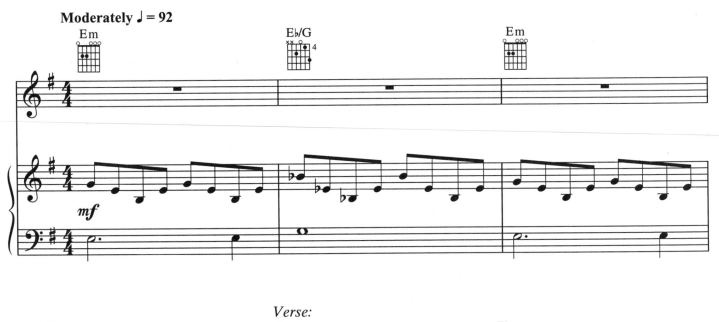

Verse:

1. It's qui-et now___ and what it brings___ is
2. *See additional lyrics*

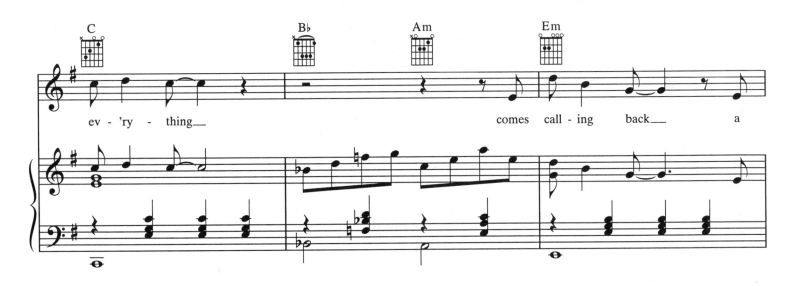

ev-'ry-thing___ comes call-ing back___ a

Leaving New York - 6 - 1
PFM0429

Verse 2:
Now, life is sweet and what it brings, I try to take.
But loneliness, it wears me out, it lies in wait.
And all not lost, still in my eye, the shadow of necklace across your thigh.
I might've lived my life in a dream, but I swear it, this is real.
Memory fuses and shatters like glass, mercurial future, forget the past.
It's you, it's what I feel.
(To Chorus:)

MAKE IT ALL OKAY

Words and Music by
PETER BUCK, MIKE MILLS, MICHAEL STIPE

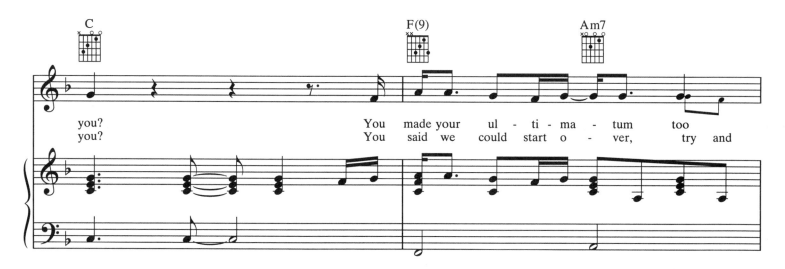

Verse 3:
Didn't you believe that I have finally turned away?
Didn't you, now? Didn't you?
Anything to hold onto to help me through my day.
Didn't you, now? Didn't you?
Jesus loves me fine,
But his words fall flat this time.
It's a long, long, long road
And I don't know which way to go.
If you offered me your world, did you think I'd really stay?
If you offered me the heavens, I would have to turn away.
Was it my imagination, or did I hear you say,
"We don't have a prayer between us"?
Didn't you, now? Didn't you, now?
Didn't you?

THE ASCENT OF MAN

Words and Music by
PETER BUCK, MIKE MILLS, MICHAEL STIPE

Moderately, with a cut time feel ♩ = 63

1. So hes-i-ta-tion pulled___ me back, I'm

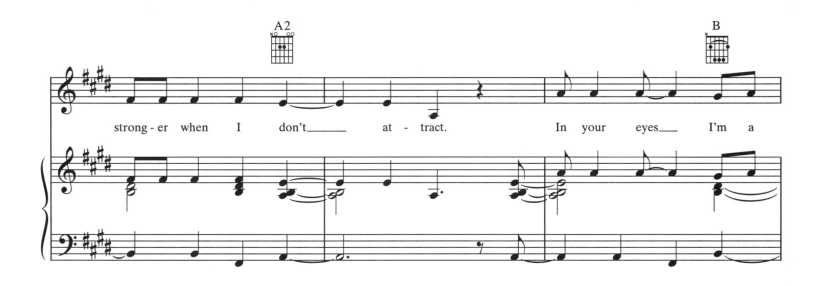

strong-er when I don't___ at-tract. In your eyes___ I'm a

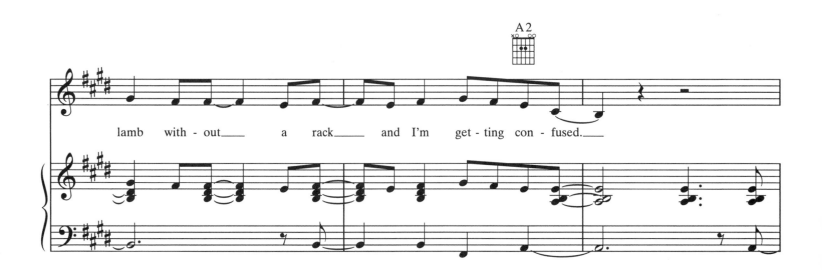

lamb with-out___ a rack___ and I'm get-ting con-fused.___

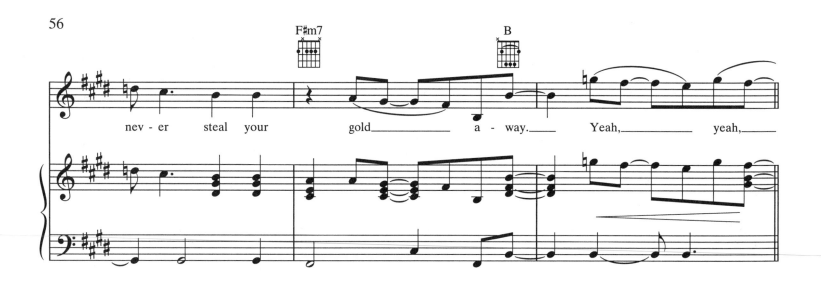

Chorus:

Verse 2:
My book is called, "The Ascent of Man."
I marked your chapter with a catamaran.
The accent's off.
But I am what I am.
(To Chorus:)

Verse 3:
I looked for you. It's my last grandstand.
A motorscootered goat-legged pan
Figure-eighting in quicksand.
(To Chorus:)

THE OUTSIDERS

Words and Music by
PETER BUCK, MIKE MILLS, MICHAEL STIPE

𝄋 *Chorus:*

Verse 2 begins:

new day is born.___ The out-sid-ers are gath-er-ing,

(Rap - See additional lyrics)

(drums)
a tempo

Repeat as needed   Last Time

Rap:
A man walks away when every muscle says to stay.
How many yesterdays? They each weigh heavy.
Who says what changes may come?
Who says what we call home?
I know you see right through me, my luminescence fades.
The dusk provides an antidote, I am not afraid.
I've been a million times in my mind
And this is really just a technicality, frailty, reality.

Uh, it's time to breathe, time to believe.
Let it go and run towards the sea.
They don't teach that, they don't know what you mean.
They don't understand, they don't know what you mean.
They don't get it, I want to scream.
I want to breathe again, I want to dream
I want to float a quote from Martin Luther King.
I am not afraid
I am not afraid
I am not afraid… etc.

WANDERLUST

Words and Music by
PETER BUCK, MIKE MILLS, MICHAEL STIPE

* Sing cue notes with Verse 2 lyric.

Wanderlust - 5 - 1
PFM0429

Chorus:

I got my sig-nals crossed.___ It's o-ver-whelm-ing be-cause_

_ I'm all a-lone and I can't get back,___ get

1. back to my wan-der-lust.___ 2. back to my wan-der, back_

___ to my wan-der, back___ to my wan-der-lust.___

THE WORST JOKE EVER

Words and Music by
PETER BUCK, MIKE MILLS, MICHAEL STIPE

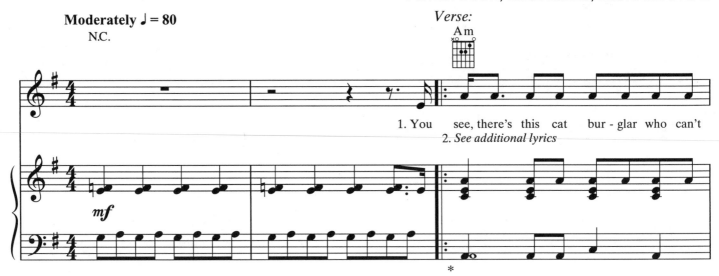

* Cue notes 2nd time.

The Worst Joke Ever - 4 - 1
PFM0429

Verse 2:
Now I am floating,
I feel released.
The moorings have been dropped,
The weights unleashed.
Everything is crystalline, simple and free.

The crime of good men who can't wrestle with change,
Or are too afraid to face this life's misjudged unknowns.
You're not hurting anybody else's chances,
But you're disfiguring your own.
(To Chorus:)